Sacagawea:
Indian Guide

Beginner
Biographies

written by M. J. Cosson   illustrated by Reed Sprunger

Content Consultant:
Richard Jensen, PhD
Author, Scholar, and Historian

magic
wagon

visit us at www.abdopublishing.com

Published by Magic Wagon, a division of the ABDO Publishing Group, 8000 West 78th Street, Edina, Minnesota 55439. Copyright © 2009 by Abdo Consulting Group, Inc. International copyrights reserved in all countries. All rights reserved. No part of this book may be reproduced in any form without written permission from the publisher.

Looking Glass Library™ is a trademark and logo of Magic Wagon.

Printed in the United States.

Text by M. J. Cosson
Illustrations by Reed Sprunger
Edited by Nadia Higgins
Interior layout and design by Emily Love
Cover design by Emily Love

Library of Congress Cataloging-in-Publication Data

Cosson, M. J.
  Sacagawea : Indian guide / by M.J. Cosson ; illustrated by Reed Sprunger.
    p. cm. — (Beginner biographies)
  Includes index.
  ISBN 978-1-60270-252-3
  1. Sacagawea—Juvenile literature. 2. Shoshoni women—Biography—Juvenile literature. 3. Shoshoni Indians—Biography—Juvenile literature. 4. Lewis and Clark Expedition (1804-1806)—Juvenile literature. I. Sprunger, Reed, ill. II. Title.
  F592.7.S123C67 2009
  978.004'9745740092—dc22
  [B]
               2008002897

Table of Contents

A Shoshone Girl

Sacagawea was born about 1788. She was a member of the Shoshone, an American Indian people. Sacagawea lived in what is now the state of Idaho.

At that time, the United States was a new country. Most people lived in cities and towns on the East Coast. The land west of the Mississippi River was very wild. It was called the frontier.

White settlers were just beginning to move to the frontier. Most of the people who lived there were Indians and fur trappers.

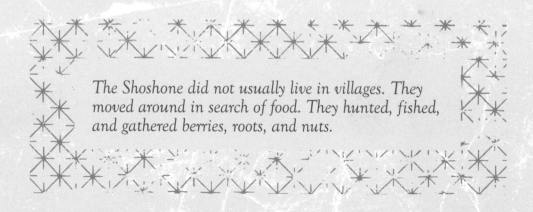

The Shoshone did not usually live in villages. They moved around in search of food. They hunted, fished, and gathered berries, roots, and nuts.

Sacagawea probably sang and danced often as a child.

Sacagawea worked
with Charbonneau.

Sacagawea's people traveled east across the Rocky Mountains. They wanted to hunt elk, deer, and buffalo. They came to a place called Three Forks.

The Hidatsa were another group of American Indians. They were enemies of the Shoshone. In 1800, the Hidatsa kidnapped Sacagawea. She lived with the Hidatsa for about a year.

Then she became the wife of a French fur trapper named Charbonneau. She was only 13 years old. Sacagawea and Charbonneau lived on the Missouri River, near the Mandan people.

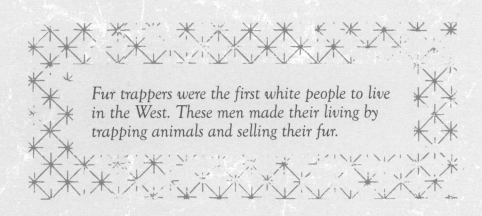

Fur trappers were the first white people to live in the West. These men made their living by trapping animals and selling their fur.

The Corps of Discovery

In 1803, Thomas Jefferson was president. He was interested in the frontier. He asked Meriwether Lewis to explore the lands out west. Lewis chose William Clark to help him. More men joined Lewis and Clark. The group was called the Corps of Discovery.

The Corps of Discovery was to explore the Louisiana Territory. The group hoped to find a water route to the Pacific Ocean.

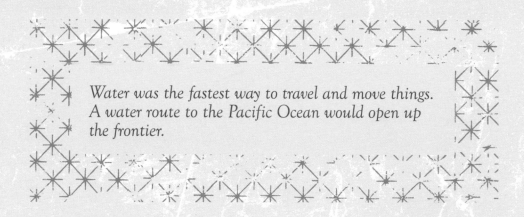

Water was the fastest way to travel and move things. A water route to the Pacific Ocean would open up the frontier.

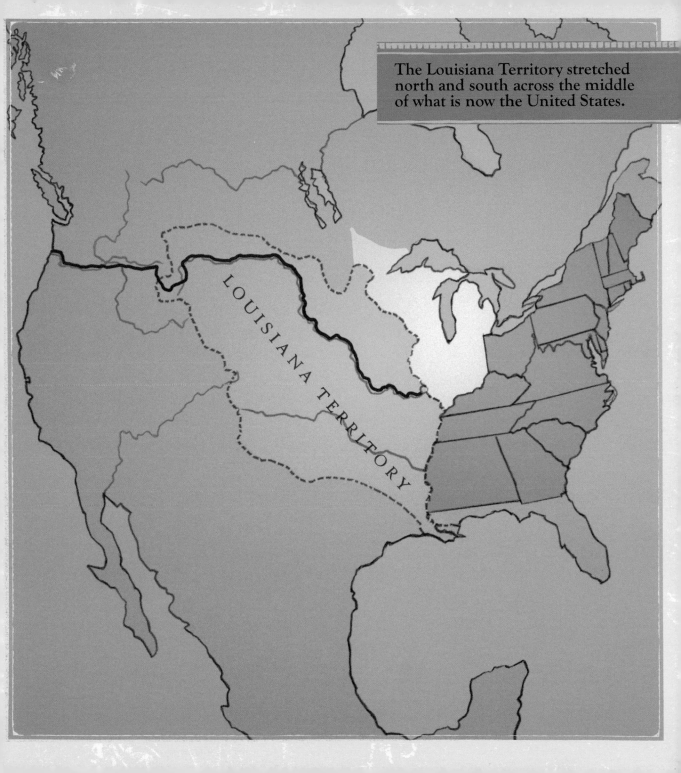

The Louisiana Territory stretched north and south across the middle of what is now the United States.

LOUISIANA TERRITORY

Lewis and Clark's expedition began in May 1804 near St. Louis, Missouri. The group traveled in boats up the Missouri River. The water was rough. So, the group traveled slowly.

In October, the group stopped for the winter. They stayed near the Mandan people on the Missouri River. There, they met Charbonneau and Sacagawea.

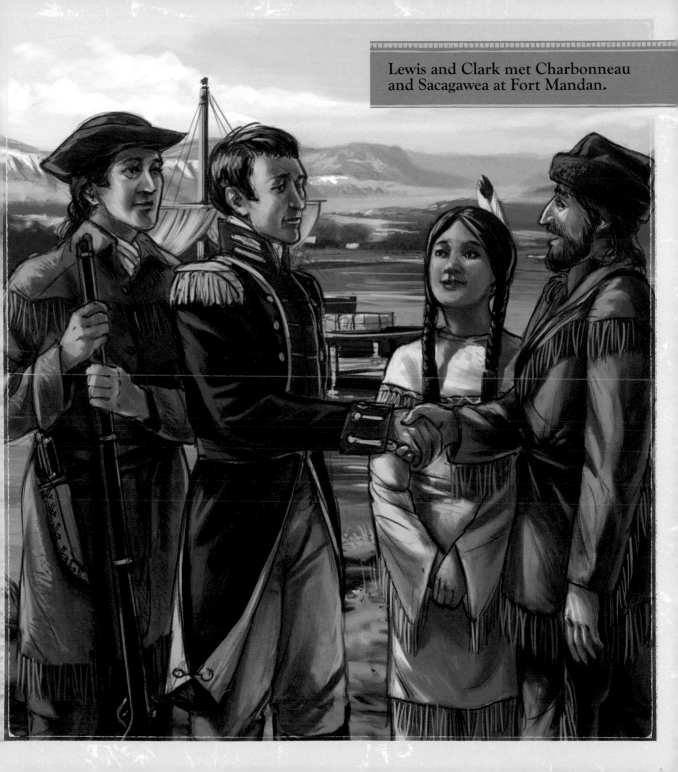

Lewis and Clark met Charbonneau and Sacagawea at Fort Mandan.

Sacagawea traveled with Pomp on her back.

Explorer and Guide

That winter Sacagawea had a baby boy. She and Charbonneau named the baby Jean-Baptiste. Everyone called him Pomp.

Lewis and Clark asked Charbonneau to come with the Corps of Discovery. They needed someone who could speak with the Indians. This person would have to translate what the Indians said.

Sacagawea and Pomp came, too. Sacagawea sat in the front of the boat with Pomp on her back. Indians who saw the group would never expect a woman to travel with soldiers. Having Sacagawea along showed the Indians that the Corps was a peaceful group.

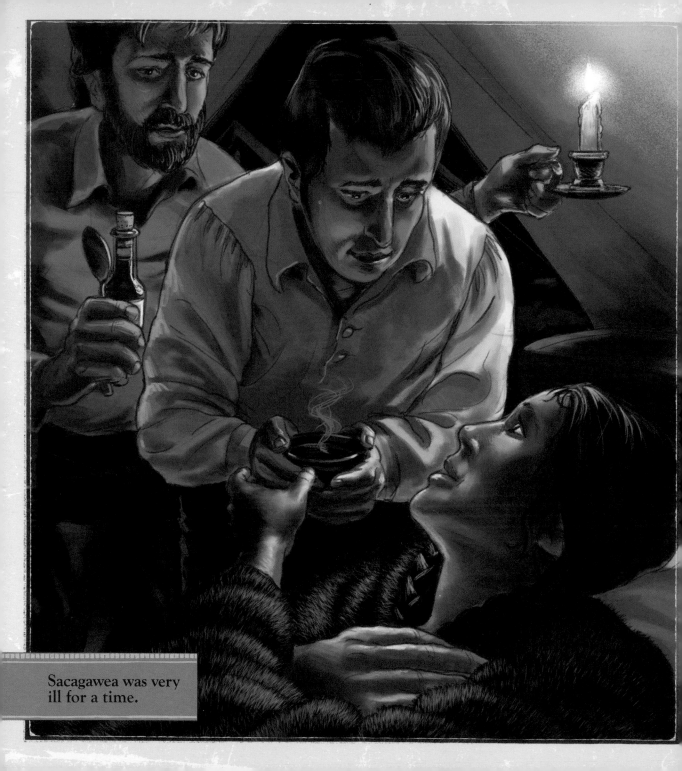

Sacagawea was very ill for a time.

Sacagawea helped the Corps with many things. She found food, such as roots and berries, that the white men did not know about. She could talk with the Shoshone people and translate for Charbonneau.

Sacagawea and the men saw many interesting and beautiful things. But the journey was not easy. The group was often cold, hungry, and tired. In June 1805, Sacagawea got very sick. Lewis and Clark gave her medicine. They had her drink a lot of water. After many days, Sacagawea got better.

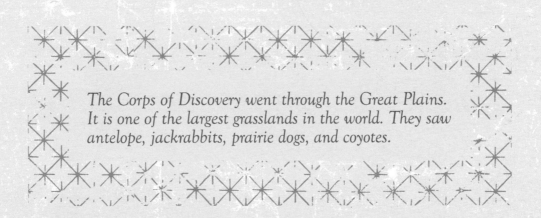

The Corps of Discovery went through the Great Plains. It is one of the largest grasslands in the world. They saw antelope, jackrabbits, prairie dogs, and coyotes.

Sacagawea rescued important journals that fell overboard.

16

An Important Rescue

The boats kept moving up the river. But as the river got smaller, it was harder to travel. At one point, the boat Sacagawea was in tipped over. Everything went in the water.

Sacagawea saved important supplies. She saved the notebooks that recorded everything about the trip. To thank her, Lewis and Clark named a river after her. *Sacagawea* means "Bird Woman." So the river became Bird Woman's River.

Sacagawea pointed out important landmarks to Lewis and Clark.

Familiar Places

In July, the Corps came to a place that looked familiar to Sacagawea. It was Three Forks, where the Hidatsa had taken her from her family.

Soon, the group came to another spot that Sacagawea recognized. She said it was close to where her people lived.

The river was becoming impossible to travel. Lewis went in search of the Shoshone. He wanted to buy horses from them. The Corps needed the horses to get over the mountains ahead.

In August, Lewis found the Shoshone chief. The chief and many Shoshone people went with Lewis to find Clark's group, including Sacagawea. When they found each other, Sacagawea recognized the chief. He was her brother!

Soon, Lewis and Clark had all the horses they needed. The Corps went on its way through the Rocky Mountains.

Sacagawea greeted her brother warmly after their years of separation.

The Corps eventually made it all the way to the Pacific Ocean.

22

To the Pacific

The Corps headed toward the Pacific Ocean through the mountains. They came across many waterfalls. They paddled down one river, then another, and another.

In November, they had to stop for the winter. Lewis and Clark held a vote. They asked each member where to set up camp. At that time, women in the United States were not allowed to vote. But Sacagawea was asked to vote on this decision! The group spent the winter at Fort Clatsop, in what is now Oregon.

Sacagawea got to see a beached whale by the Pacific Ocean.

Sacagawea was amazed by the sights along the coast. One day, the men were going to the ocean to see a beached whale. Sacagawea had never asked for anything. But now she asked to go see the whale. She went along and saw the huge creature. She also saw the ocean for the first time.

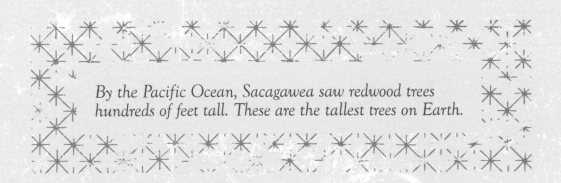

By the Pacific Ocean, Sacagawea saw redwood trees hundreds of feet tall. These are the tallest trees on Earth.

On the return trip, Lewis saw a beautiful fur robe. He wanted to give it to President Jefferson. Sacagawea always wore a belt of blue beads. She got the robe for Lewis by trading her belt for it. For this and many reasons, Lewis and Clark were glad that Sacagawea had come along.

Sacagawea presented the fur robe to Lewis.

Remembering Sacagawea

Sacagawea traveled with the Corps for almost a year and a half. She and her family returned home to the Mandan village in August 1806.

Six years later, Sacagawea had a daughter named Lisette. Sacagawea had been sick for many years. She died at the age of 25 on December 22, 1812.

Today, Sacagawea is shown on a U.S. dollar coin. That is just one way she is remembered for her important role in the Lewis and Clark expedition.

FUN FACTS

✦ Sacagawea went by many names. As a child, she was called Grass Maiden. Lewis and Clark often called her Janey because it was easy to say.

✦ Sacagawea spoke the Shoshone language. She translated to Hidatsa. Charbonneau translated the Hidatsa to French. A Corps member translated the French to English. Then Lewis and Clark knew what the Shoshone people had said.

✦ After Sacagawea died, Clark adopted Pomp and Lisette. No one is sure what happened to Lisette. Pomp went to school. At 18, he traveled in Europe with a German prince.

TIMELINE

Around 1788 Sacagawea was born.

1800 Sacagawea was kidnapped by the Hidatsa.

1801 Sacagawea married Charbonneau.

1805 Pomp was born in February.

1805 Sacagawea and her family joined the Corps of Discovery in the spring.

1805 Sacagawea was reunited with her brother in August.

1805 Some members of the Corps reached the Pacific Ocean on November 7.

1806 Sacagawea and her family returned home in the summer.

1812 Lisette was born.

1812 Sacagawea died on December 22.

GLOSSARY

Corps of Discovery—the group of men and one woman who went on Lewis and Clark's expedition.

expedition—a trip by a group of people to explore a new place.

frontier—the border between settled land and wilderness.

Louisiana Territory—a huge area of land in the middle of the United States that stretched west of the Mississippi River.

translate—to take something in a different language and put it into one's own language.

water route—a way to travel by water.

LEARN MORE

At the Library

Adler, David. *A Picture Book of Sacagawea*. New York: Holiday House, 2001.

Krensky, Stephen. *Sacagawea and the Bravest Deed*. New York: Aladdin, 2002.

Petrie, Kristin. *Sacagawea*. Explorers. Edina: ABDO Publishing, 2007.

Tieck, Sarah. *Sacagawea*. First Biographies. Edina: ABDO Publishing, 2007.

On the Web

To learn more about Sacagawea, visit ABDO Publishing Company on the World Wide Web at **www.abdopublishing.com**. Web sites about Sacagawea are featured on our Book Links page. These links are routinely monitored and updated to provide the most current information available.

INDEX